JOURNAL TO THE SOUL

THE ART OF SACRED JOURNAL KEEPING

ROSE OFFNER

This book belongs to

_____

It is my private journal.
Please do not read it without my permission.
Thank you for honoring my request.

GIBBS·SMITH
PUBLISHER

SALT LAKE CITY

FIRST EDITION

99 98 97 96   5 4 3 2 1

Text and art © 1996 by Rose Offner

Photographs copyright as noted:
Freddo Blumberg, copyright © 1996 *Legs
Sticking Out of the Tub*; Andy Frascheski,
copyright © 1996, *Body of the Woman*;
Monica Hellburg, copyright © 1996, *Door*.

Art by Caroll Shreeve, *Once Upon a Time
Dragon with Castle and Hut*, copyright © 1996
by Rose Offner

This is a Peregrine Smith Book, published by
Gibbs Smith, Publisher
P.O. Box 667
Layton, Utah 84041

Designed and composed by Kinde Nebeker
Edited by Caroll Shreeve
Printed and bound in Singapore

ISBN 0-87905-702-5

ACKNOWLEDGMENTS

With sincere and heartfelt gratitude, I wish to thank Gibbs Smith, my publisher, for taking a risk and being the visionary that you are. I am grateful for your support, encouragement, and belief in me. Most of all, I thank you for making my life's dream a reality.

To Caroll Shreeve, my editor at Gibbs Smith, for visualizing this journal the way I described it and walking me through my fears. Thanks for taking time to write to me and encourage me when I really needed it. Thanks to Madge Baird, editorial director at Gibbs Smith, for being there when I had questions and needed answers, and for your expertise in guiding us all. To all the Gibbs Smith team for what you are doing and what you will be doing, I appreciate and thank you all.

To Kinde Nebeker, my designer, who gave her talent and professional skill to create and design the composition and topography for this journal. I thank you for going out of your way to make my art even more beautiful.

Thanks to my friends and professional colleagues who graciously shared their time, energy, and talent: Christopher Van Buren, author and friend, who saw the writer in me and guided me in the pursuit of writing and publishing. Sally Richards, thank you for your inspiring class, encouragement, support, and friendship. Jack Newton for your guidance, encouragement, company, and help whenever I needed it. Jack and Janet at Southbay Software for your constant support and professional services. Dave Guillmett for your expert computer and organizational skills. Bill Melcher for your computer help and personal time. Debi Fernandez for assistance, support, and generously opening your home for my workshop sessions. Thanks to all my teachers and students who have believed in my work and set me on the author path.

Without the love, support, and constant encouragement of my friends, I could not have brought my dream journal to reality. Thank you all; I love you and appreciate your friendship in my life more than words can say: Janna and Paul, Lois Arigotti, Peter Scarsdale, Gail, Michael Fogli, Steven Jamison, Colleen Holden, and Frank Coppell. A special heartfelt thanks to Wendy McLaughlin and Barry for being my friends. I love you.

And my best friend in the whole world, Anne Taddei, for always, always being there, for listening to me read all my books aloud, and most of all for giving me the gift of laughter. Thanks to you, my life is always so much lighter.

I want to thank my Mom for giving me the gift of life and enduring with me while I pursued my dreams. To Rich Srsen, thanks for being family and supporting my dream and vision. To all of my family, my brothers and sisters: Trish, Bev, Vicky, Zeke, and Arron, and my brothers-and-sisters-in-law, my nieces and nephews—I love you all.

My greatest inspiration in life has been my daughter, Danielle, who has always been willing to make sacrifices while I pursued my dreams. Thanks, Sweetie.

Most of all, I wish to thank the Creator for using me. Thank you, God, for allowing me to serve.

*A*S WE TELL OUR STORIES, WE HEAL.

'STORY' REACHES A PLACE
DEEP IN THE SOUL
THAT MERE WORDS CANNOT REACH.

YOUR STORY IS IMPORTANT.

YOUR JOURNAL
IS YOUR LIVING AUTOBIOGRAPHY.

Journal to the Soul is a beautiful interactive journal, a unique mixture of self-help and art meant to inspire each reader to capture the sacred journey of his or her life. You are guided in the art and exploration of keeping a cherished journal. Each page holds colorful and meaningful art, rich in beauty and symbols that encourage the writing process. You will list your top 100 dreams on pages filled with blue sky and clouds—embodying the image of dreams and reaching for the sky. Throughout the book, artistic images draw more from each transformational process. The unique pocket and envelope images inspire you to make places to save treasures of love as well as to record and store negative thoughts and feelings in a brown paper bag, and then to throw them away. This journal is a special place for you to write—carefully designed with explanations of each process, organized to draw the most out of the reader's journaling process. You become the writer of your own personal story.

CONTENTS

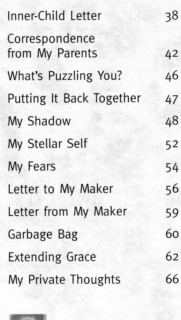

HOW TO USE THIS JOURNAL

Keeping a journal is a healing art. Writing about your life, challenges, past, and present is a way to gain clarity about who you are. Journals later remind you of past mistakes and can save you from repeating them. This book was created with love, heart, and soul. It was conceived, illustrated, and designed to be beautiful to remind you of your inner beauty. Beauty is an element of soul. Color, imagery, art, and metaphor have healing power.

Privacy is very important, so don't leave your journal out where someone might be tempted to read it. Its beauty will attract exploration. Journals allow us to express ourselves from the heart and can assist us in finding and expressing our creativity. *Journal to the Soul* was designed with pages where you can create your own beautiful pockets and envelopes or design your own stationary. I hope you will take the time to play and have fun finding and expressing yourself and your creativity.

It is really fun to be able to cut, glue, and create your own pockets and envelopes, and to design your own stationary. We are all creative. Have fun. This is a place where you can allow the child inside you to play.

There are some great supplies available to make your creative experience with this journal even more fun. My favorite envelopes are made by Strathmore out of beautiful watercolor paper. They have a great texture, if you like that quality. They can be found in most stationary and art supply stores. You can also use any envelopes or make your own from gift wrap, wallpaper, or any paper that pleases you. You can decorate them with Crayola Changeables™ or overwriters of any brand—pastels, watercolors, markers, collage effects, and colored pencils. When I didn't have any money for art supplies, I used old envelopes and beautiful wrapping paper that I cut into strips and glued around the borders of my journal to make it look like a storybook. I created the envelopes with collage images I cut from mailers, magazines, greeting cards, stickers—whatever pleased me and looked special. I love gold ink on my borders, so I use a gold pen to make my journal more sacred and beautiful. Metallic pens also come in silver and copper. Sometimes metallic pens leak, so be careful. But even then, some of my favorite art came from what I at first thought were my mistakes.

If you don't have enough writing space, continue on another piece of paper and make a pocket somewhere in your journal for these extra pages. I have a black envelope for angry feelings and private thoughts and a white envelope for processes I feel I've completed to my satisfaction.

Having pockets and envelopes in your journal adds a wonderful dimension to your journal keeping. They give you sacred places to store the mementos you cherish. You can also make pockets by cutting a strong piece of gift wrap or construction paper in half and gluing its bottom and sides to the bottom of the journal page. Avoid gluing pockets and envelopes shut.

IDEAS FOR USING POCKETS AND ENVELOPES

Since journals chronicle our lives, it is wonderful to be able to store our deep feelings and cherished mementos. Remember to leave the top edge of your pockets open to receive your secret writings. The following process pocket and envelope suggestions can be added to with others you choose to make throughout your journal:

UNSENT LETTER POCKET: A place to keep letters that you write to others expressing your true feelings. Allow yourself to say all that you desire. Unsent letters may be written to those with whom you are angry but with whom it would be inappropriate to fully express your angry feelings. You may write to the deceased, to God, your higher power, or your guardian angel.

LOVE POCKET: A place to save very special letters or cards that you cherish, to reread at times when you want to remind yourself you are loved.

GARBAGE BAG: A place to write about and then throw away negativity, including negative thoughts, feelings, doubts, and fears that may be holding you back from becoming whole.

PERSONAL POCKET: A place to put private or dark thoughts, things you might not want to mar the beauty of your journal. A place to write about your anger, hurt, or disappointments or anything that is particularly private.

ANGER POCKET: A place to write about your anger and to face, explore, and then release unresolved anger. When you are ready to let it go, release it, or forgive, then you can throw it away or burn it.

TREASURE POCKET: A place to keep special keepsakes and cherished mementos.

This book can be used in any way you desire. You can experience it in the order it is presented or open it to a random page and begin writing. You may find yourself wanting to jump around. You might do an exercise that is deep and evocative and then choose to do a closing process that is lighter and more uplifting. The pages that you want to resist doing most are typically the ones that you would benefit by doing first. It is not uncommon to want to put off facing something that may be uncomfortable. That is where having the heart of a warrior comes in. It is only in our courage to face life with a tender heart that we can move through our resistance and experience true joy and happiness.

SELF-INQUIRY

In order to live authentically, you must first be who you are in life and know who you are. Realizing and actualizing your true self is one of the greatest gifts you can give yourself and others. Begin with self-inquiry, telling your birth story and why you were born, naming your values, telling your life story. It has been said that as you share your story, a healing begins. Thus, you are guided home to your true self, to the divine that resides within you.

SELF-HEALING FROM ANGER AND FORGIVENESS

In order to be truly liberated, to be who you are in life, it is imperative that you face your anger and the wounds that may be holding you back from having healthy relationships with yourself and with others. It is impossible to be truly happy until you face and then release yourself from past burdens. Facing your own shadow, the dark parts of yourself you try to hide, is a way to identify and heal past wounds. Then, to forgive yourself and others, to extend grace and compassion may bring tears as you open your heart and allow yourself to experience love and healing—from the inside out. Welcome your tears, for they are Life's longing to express through you, to heal, and to wash the wounds and disappointments of your soul. Your tears are balm for your soul; they soothe you and bring you closer to the truth.

SELF-ESTEEM
THE ART OF SELF-LOVE

Think of your journal as a cherished friend, in fact a best friend; it can be there for you any time of day or night. When you talk, it will listen and hear your deepest whispers and soothe your soul.

When you were a child and would go exploring, you were taught to take a friend and stick together. If you didn't, you were bound to get in trouble. The buddy system has always been encouraged in scouting and adult adventuring in the outdoors. Self-exploration can be exciting and scary. When going into the recesses of yourself, you face your darkness and your light; it is important to remember as you begin your journey into the depths of your heart that you are not alone. You can call upon God, spirit, your guide, or higher power for strength and guidance. Writing can create an opening in the heart, a tender vulnerability that allows you to bring up forgotten memories and make conscious what was hidden even from yourself. Vulnerability can bring forth tears and then tremendous joy as you break through your personal blocks, becoming your true self and honoring the divinity that

resides within. Balance in life comes about when you are living your connection with your mind, body, and spirit.

SELF-FULFILLMENT
MANIFESTING YOUR DREAMS
AND HEART'S DESIRES

To manifest means "to make evident or plainly show something." You can manifest your dreams by clearly knowing and stating what you desire. Positive expectation, a heartfelt belief, and picturing it or visualizing it in your mind, move you closer to the fulfillment of your dreams. You must first move through the obstacles you have created for yourself. Action moves you out of your resistance. Once you let go of your resistance, your dreams can come true. Making lists of your dreams and desires helps you to gain clarity, to know what you want in life. Knowing who you are, facing your shadow and your past, moves you to a place of self-acceptance and love. To love and be loved you must first love and forgive yourself and others. Writing and creative expression are vehicles for finding your voice, healing your past, and manifesting your dreams. As you express your true self with love, your resistance melts, and you magnetically attract your dreams and heart's desires.

This book is especially for you who long for a beautiful place to write your truth and who desire to make writing fun and meaningful. It is a gift you give yourself. It is also a gift you give those you love. Use your imagination on any extra pages to create your own exercises and art.

ONCE UPON A TIME . . .

Write about your life or a piece of your life that you don't understand and would like to. Write it as a fairy tale or short story. Begin your story with, "Once upon a time . . ." or "It was told that . . ." Include an obstacle that has yet to be overcome, an encounter that has significance, the gift you received or the lesson learned, and how you came to triumph in the end.

MY SELF-PORTRAIT

Write about who you were . . . who you are . . . and who you will be . . . or write about your "True Self" and how you became who you are.

POSTCARD TO LIFE

Write a thank-you note to God, your higher power, or life. Express your gratitude. It is said that whatever we are grateful for increases in our lives.

AIR MAIL

LIFE'S SACRED QUESTION

lose your eyes, take a deep breath, and exhale slowly. Ceremoniously and from your heart, ask the sacred question of Life: "What do you want me to do next?" Listen from that quiet place deep in your heart. Open your eyes, and begin to write about the response you hear. Whenever we ask in this sacred fashion, Life hears us and responds. Answers will often come in a one-word phrase form or short succinct sentences. We often have the answers within; all we have to do is trust our inner voice.

SACRED ANSWERS

Write your imagined sacred response from Life, and place it
in an envelope or pocket you create and glue here.

MY BIRTH STORY

Write about your birth story and why you were born. Begin with "I was born . . ."

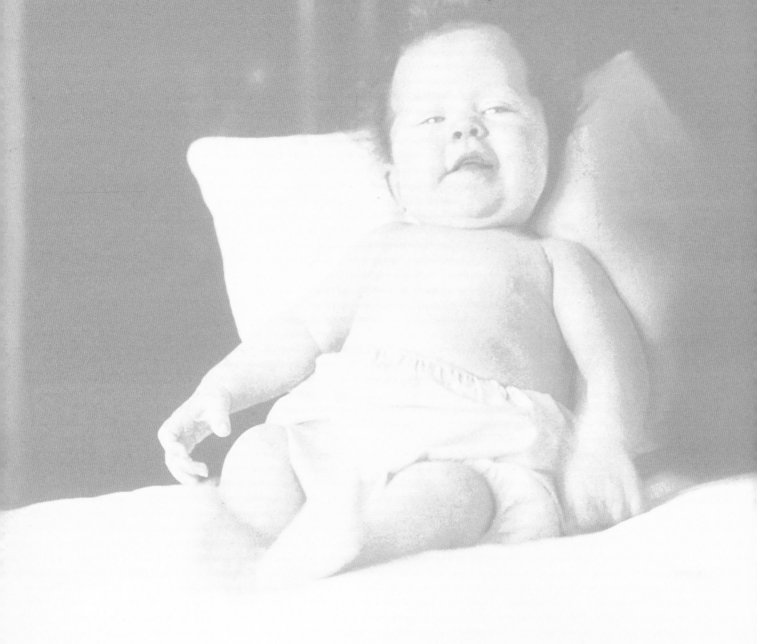

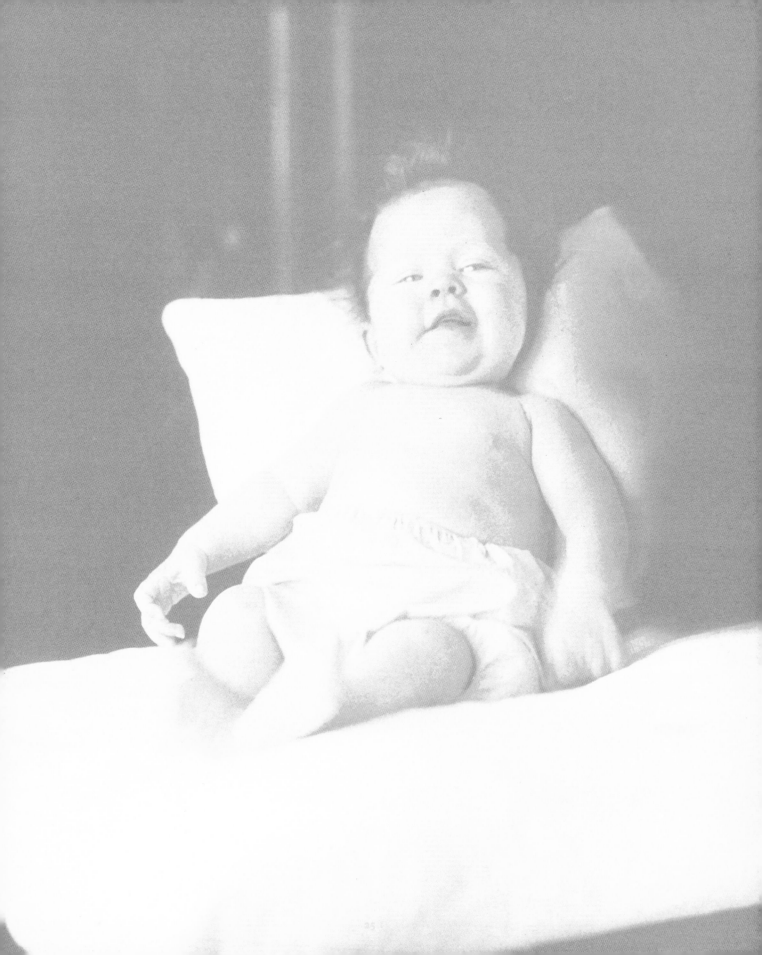

BODY TALK

The body houses the soul. Write about your relationship with your body. Do you love or abuse your body? Write about what you could do or are already doing to have a healthy relationship with your body.

LIFE'S VALUES

Clarify your values. List your seven to ten most important values in life; then ask yourself if you are living your life in accordance with your values. What changes can you make so that what you value and the way you are living your life will match?

MY FEELINGS

Write of your most frequently felt feelings. Remember, we are the ones who choose. Write about what you would like to be feeling and what you are willing to do to create those feelings.

MY LIFE'S CREED

Write a sacred creed for your life. Write about your intentions and commitment to each role you play in life as a friend, parent, daughter, son, etc. The creed we live by is our mission or code in life. It is a succinct way of stating our intentions to fulfill our desired life results.

REMEMBERING

Write about what you remember from either your childhood, young adulthood, or any time. Remembering is a part of healing, a part of understanding. As you begin to write, you may remember things you thought you forgot or have wanted to forget. In the telling there is healing. Include what you saw, felt, heard—all of it. Bring it to life. If it is a painful memory, visualize bringing your adult self with you as you go back to that time. Have your adult self do or say whatever you needed at that time to take care of yourself.

INNER-CHILD LETTER

Holding a big primary pencil or a crayon, use your less-dominant hand and write a letter to one or both of your parents. Begin "Dear Mom" or "Dear Dad" (or whatever names you used for your parents). See what comes.

CORRESPONDENCE
FROM MY PARENTS

In a letter to yourself from your parents, write all the things you've always wanted to hear them say and never did. With an open heart, allow your past to be healed. Listen carefully and write from your heart; imagine you hear their voices as you write.

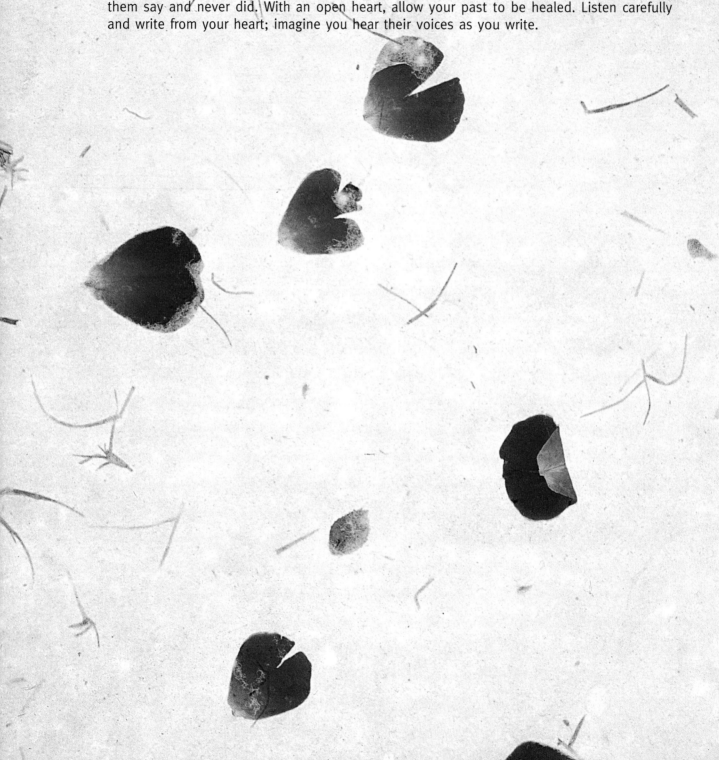

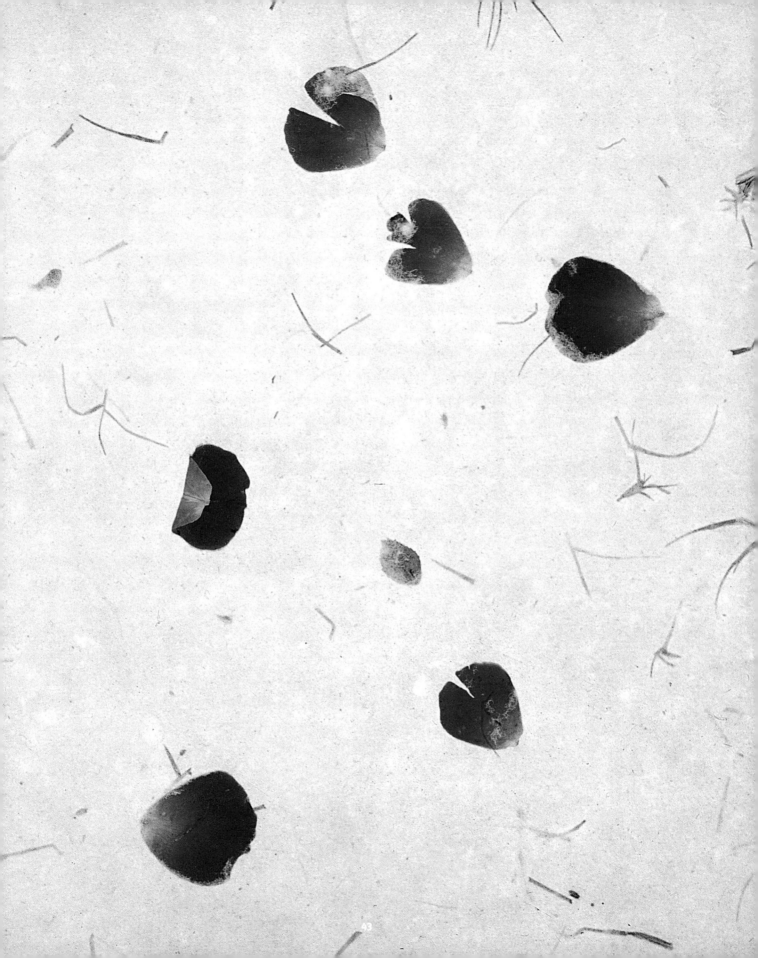

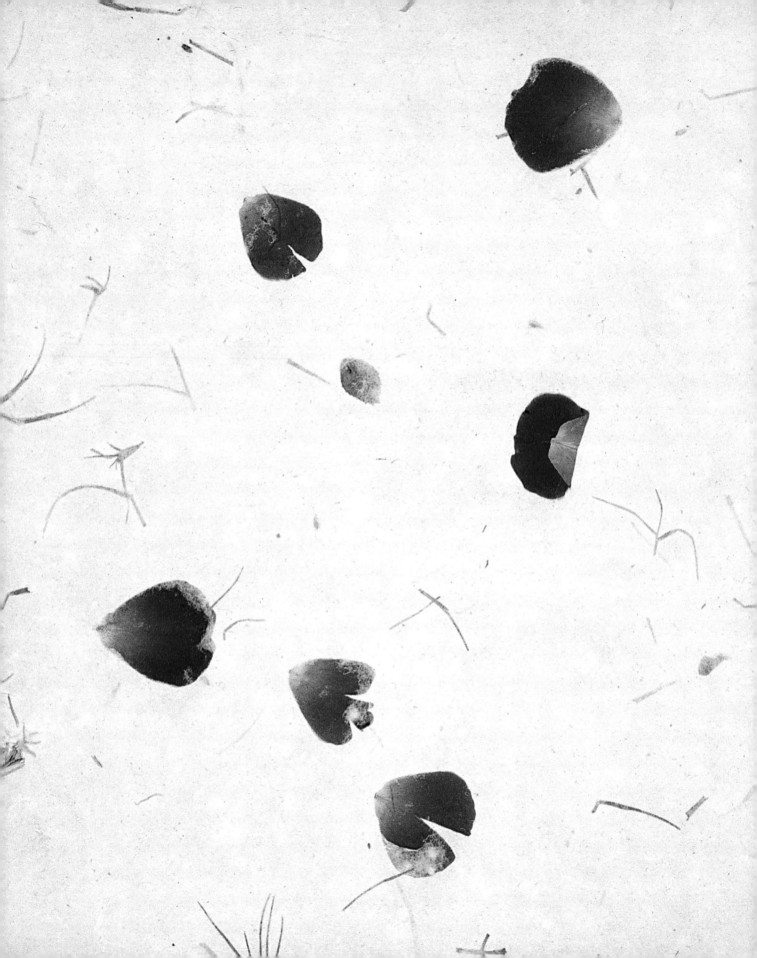

WHAT'S PUZZLING YOU?

Write about the puzzling challenges in each piece of your life. Or write about the parts of your life that you don't understand. Include your home life, career or school, relationships, personal matters, time spent, etc.

PUTTING IT BACK TOGETHER

For each puzzling piece of your life that challanges you, write about the thought, action, or belief you would need to change in order to bring about the solution you desire.

MY SHADOW

Write about your dark side—the parts of yourself you don't want anyone to know about, the parts you try to hide from yourself and others.

CREATE YOUR OWN ENVELOPE OR POCKET
FOR YOUR DARK OR PRIVATE THOUGHTS TO GLUE HERE.

MY STELLAR SELF

Where do you shine in your life? Write about the special gifts you bring to life—the talents or skills you share. What talents and skills do you desire that you've yet to discover or develop?

MY FEARS

Make a list of your fears. Acknowledging your fears is one step toward releasing you from their power. Each time you overcome a fear, you free up energy you can use positively in another area of your life.

LETTER TO MY MAKER

Write a letter to God, your Maker, or Higher Power about an area in your life you are having difficulty with. Close your eyes, take a deep breath, go into that quiet place within, and imagine that you receive a letter from God, your Higher Power, or Spirit. Listen, and begin to write and to receive what comes with an open heart.

LETTER FROM MY MAKER

Write and receive an imagined response from your maker. Place it in an envelope or pocket you create and glue here.

GARBAGE BAG

Make a garbage-bag pocket from a brown paper bag, and glue it here. "Throw away" all that is getting in the way of your fulfilled and happy life. Write about the garbage you carry from the past or present. Include your doubts, fears, and negative thoughts.

EXTENDING GRACE

Forgiveness is one of the most important lessons we can learn in life. As we forgive, so we are forgiven. Write about what forgiveness means to you, about what not forgiving is costing you, about what you have yet to forgive yourself for.

MY PRIVATE THOUGHTS

This is the place to write about all of the personal and private things you don't want anyone to read. Safely tuck them into a pocket or envelope that you create and glue here.

NURTURING MYSELF

What can you do to nurture yourself ? What acts of kindness, relaxation, or gifts of fun do you—and could you—bestow upon yourself ? List all the ways you currently nurture yourself, or new ways you have yet to experience. Perhaps a massage, a good book, a facial, a day to yourself . . .

LETTER FROM LIFE

Writing from your heart, listen and receive a letter from the Spirit of Life thanking you for your contributions. Begin the letter "Dear _____ we appreciate you for . . ."

(your name)

"Love, the Spirit of Life"

CREATE YOUR OWN ENVELOPE AND GLUE IT HERE.

CREATING BALANCE

Where is your life out of balance? Write about the actions, thoughts, or beliefs you need to change to create balance in your life.

LIFE AWARDS YOU

Give yourself an award that you truly deserve
for being a good mom or dad, a best friend, a survivor . . .

Certificate of Award

In honor and recognition of your fine performance,
we hereby present

_____

(your name)

With this Certificate of Award for

_____

_____

_____

On this _____ day of _____ 19__

Your Maker

MY LIFE'S SUCCESSES

Write about what success means to you and how you'll know when you've reached it. What is your criteria for success? List the accomplishments you've achieved. Include areas of your life where you have grown, loved, forgiven; relationships you've healed; and the simple things you feel proud of.

100 DREAMS

List 100 dreams and desires you have. Write about what you yearn for. Name your heart's desires, and include specific items: work or career, family and home, personal and spiritual goals, dreams you have for those you love and for the world. Remember that Life hears you and responds. To get what you want in life, you must first know what it is. As your dreams come to pass, remember to check them off here. It is empowering to know you can create that which you desire.

1. _____ ☐
2. _____ ☐
3. _____ ☐
4. _____ ☐
5. _____ ☐
6. _____ ☐
7. _____ ☐
8. _____ ☐
9. _____ ☐
10. _____ ☐
11. _____ ☐
12. _____ ☐
13. _____ ☐
14. _____ ☐
15. _____ ☐
16. _____ ☐
17. _____ ☐
18. _____ ☐
19. _____ ☐
20. _____ ☐
21. _____ ☐

22._____ ☐
23._____ ☐
24._____ ☐
25._____ ☐
26._____ ☐
27._____ ☐
28._____ ☐
29._____ ☐
30._____ ☐
31._____ ☐
32._____ ☐
33._____ ☐
34._____ ☐
35._____ ☐
36._____ ☐
37._____ ☐
38._____ ☐
39._____ ☐
40._____ ☐
41._____ ☐
42._____ ☐
43._____ ☐
44._____ ☐
45._____ ☐
46._____ ☐
47._____ ☐
48._____ ☐

49. _____ ☐
50. _____ ☐
51. _____ ☐
52. _____ ☐
53. _____ ☐
54. _____ ☐
55. _____ ☐
56. _____ ☐
57. _____ ☐
58. _____ ☐
59. _____ ☐
60. _____ ☐
61. _____ ☐
62. _____ ☐
63. _____ ☐
64. _____ ☐
65. _____ ☐
66. _____ ☐
67. _____ ☐
68. _____ ☐
69. _____ ☐
70. _____ ☐
71. _____ ☐
72. _____ ☐
73. _____ ☐
74. _____ ☐
75. _____ ☐

76._____ ☐
77._____ ☐
78._____ ☐
79._____ ☐
80._____ ☐
81._____ ☐
82._____ ☐
83._____ ☐
84._____ ☐
85._____ ☐
86._____ ☐
87._____ ☐
88._____ ☐
89._____ ☐
90._____ ☐
91._____ ☐
92._____ ☐
93._____ ☐
94._____ ☐
95._____ ☐
96._____ ☐
97._____ ☐
98._____ ☐
99._____ ☐
100._____ ☐

FUTURE VISIONING

Write about your vision for your future. Write about the life you would like to be living and what you will be experiencing in your life one to five years from today. Write it affirmatively as though it were already so.

ADVENTURING

Life is an adventure. Write about an adventure you have had or would like to experience, or a spontaneous act of fun you would enjoy. You may even write about a fantasy adventure you've dreamed of having. Describe everything in rich detail.

MONEY TALKS

Write about your relationship with money . . . or write a letter to Money expressing your desire for a healthy relationship with financial comfort or success and what you could do to create that now.

AWAKENING CREATIVITY

Complete the following sentences:

If I were more creative . . .

In my life I am creative when I . . .

What blocks me from expressing my creativity is . . .

What I could do to awaken my creativity is . . .

DOORWAYS TO THE SOUL

Write about the doors that are opening or closing in your life.

BOOKS THAT HAVE INSPIRED ME

The Artist's Way:
A spiritual path to
higher creativity
Julia Cameron

Bridge of Light
Launa Nuffines

The Brothers Karamazov
Dostoyevsky

The Creative Journal
Lucia Capacchione

Creative Visualization
Shakti Gawain

Crime and Punishment
Dostoyevsky

The Dynamic Laws of
Prosperity:
My Favorite Fiction
Catherine Ponder

Focusing
Eugene Gendlin

The Glass Bead Game
Herman Hesse

Handbook for the Soul
Richard Carlson and
Benjamin Shield, eds.

If You Want to Write
Brenda Ueland

Inevitable Grace
Piero Ferrucci

Journal to the Self
Kathleen Adams

Life's Companion:
Journal Writing as a
Spiritual Quest
Christina Baldwin

Living with Joy
Sanaya Roman

A Path with Heart
Jack Kornfield

The Prophet
Kahlil Gibran

A Return to Love
Marianne Williamson

The Secret Language
of Symbols
Fontana

The 7 Habits of Highly
Effective People
Stephen R. Covey

Shambala
Chogyam Trungpa

Siddhartha
Herman Hesse

Their Eyes Were
Watching God
Nora Zeale Hurston

Writing Down the Bones
Natalie Goldberg

What We May Be
Piero Ferrucci

Women Who Run
with Wolves
Clarissa Pinkola Estes

FEEL FREE TO USE THIS PAGE FOR GLUING ON A POCKET OR ENVELOPE.
For information regarding Rose Offner's books, tapes, lectures,
workshops, and consulting arrangements, contact:

FROM THE INSIDE OUT
2030 Pioneer Court
San Mateo, CA 94403
(415) 571-6251

Blank (full-color) Journal to accompany Journal to the Soul *available soon.*